CONTENTS

1 Operations with Whole Numbers

Workout 1

Do the calculation.

①	②	③	④
3 7 1 2 6 9 5 4 8 + 7 6 3	2 7 3 x 4 6	19 ⟌ 4 3 7	85 ⟌ 1 2 7 5

⑤   913 + 685 + 427 = _____   ⑥   25 308 – 8273   = _____

⑦   16 420 – 9586   = _____   ⑧   802 + 198 + 567   = _____

⑨   308 x 69   = _____   ⑩   7266 ÷ 42   = _____

⑪   6458 ÷ 74   = _____   ⑫   694 x 58   = _____

⑬   30 028 – 7963   = _____   ⑭   8026 ÷ 96   = _____

Workout 2

Calculate. Use the correct order of operations.

⑮ $4 \times 12 - 9$ = _____

⑯ $126 \div 6 - 4$ = _____

⑰ $48 - 15 \times 2$ = _____

⑱ $57 - 9 \div 3$ = _____

⑲ $25 + 100 \div 5$ = _____

⑳ $16 + 4 \times 7$ = _____

㉑ $27 + 3 \times 16 \div 6$ = _____

㉒ $12 + 18 \div 3 \times 4$ = _____

㉔ $55 - 10 \div 5 + 5$ = _____

㉖ $65 - 12 \times 2 + 3$ = _____

Reminder

Order of operations:

1st   Do all multiplication and division in order from left to right.

2nd   Do all addition and subtraction in order from left to right.

    $12 - 4 \times 2$ $12 - 4 \times 2$
    $= 8 \times 2$ $= 12 - 8$
    $= 16$ ✗ $= 4$ ✔

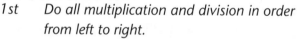

㉓ $60 - 24 \div 6 + 2 \times 3$ = _____

㉕ $20 + 8 \div 4 - 2 \times 6$ = _____

㉗ $120 \div 5 - 3 \times 6$ = _____

Workout 3

The children are helping in the library. Solve their problems and show your work.

㉘ 1152 non-fiction books are put on 16 bookshelves equally. How many books are on each bookshelf?

_____ books are on each bookshelf.

㉙ There are 552 picture books in the library. If the average cost of each book is $18, what is the total cost of the picture books?

The total cost of the picture books is $_____ .

㉚ There are 300 reference books in all. 48 big books are shelved on a special bookcase. The rest are put on bookshelves with 27 books on each shelf. How many bookshelves are needed for the rest of the books?

_____ bookshelves are needed for the rest of the books.

㉛ There are 828 fiction books. Some are put on 7 shelves with 36 books each. The rest are put on 12 bookshelves equally. How many books are on each of these 12 bookshelves?

_____ books are on each bookshelf.

EXTRA Workout

Help the library teacher find the answers.

㉜ There are totally _____ library books in the school.

㉝ To divide all library books equally among 12 classes in the school, each class will have _____ library books, including _____ non-fiction books, _____ picture books, _____ reference books, and _____ fiction books.

② Number Theory

Workout 1

Use the 50-square chart to complete the following questions.

① Colour the multiples of 2 red.

② Circle the multiples of 3.

③ Cross ✖ the multiples of 5.

④ Put a △ on the multiples of 8.

1	2	3	4	5	6	7	8	9	10
11	12	13	14	15	16	17	18	19	20
21	22	23	24	25	26	27	28	29	30
31	32	33	34	35	36	37	38	39	40
41	42	43	44	45	46	47	48	49	50

Refer to ① – ④. List the common multiples up to 50 for each group of numbers and write their least common multiple (L.C.M.).

		Common multiples	L.C.M.
⑤	2 and 3		
⑥	3 and 5		
⑦	2, 3 and 8		

Workout 2

Complete the multiplication or division sentences. Then list all the factors of each number.

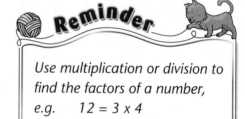

Reminder

Use multiplication or division to find the factors of a number,
e.g.   12 = 3 x 4
12 ÷ 3= 4
3 and 4 are factors of 12.

⑧ 18 = 1 x _____

  = 2 x _____

  = 3 x _____

⑨ 28 ÷ 1 = _____

  28 ÷ 2 = _____

  28 ÷ 4 = _____

⑩ 36 = 1 x _____

  = 2 x _____

  = 3 x _____

  = 4 x _____

  = 6 x _____

⑪ 48 ÷ 1 = _____

  48 ÷ 2 = _____

  48 ÷ 3 = _____

  48 ÷ 4 = _____

  48 ÷ 6 = _____

⑫

	Factors
18	
28	
36	
48	

Refer to ⑫. List the common factors of each group of numbers and fill in their greatest common factor (G.C.F.).

⑬ 28 and 36   Common factors _____   G.C.F. = _____

⑭ 18 and 48   Common factors _____   G.C.F. = _____

⑮ 28, 36 and 48   Common factors _____   G.C.F. = _____

 **Workout 3**

Circle the prime numbers.

 **Reminder**

⑯

2	5	15	23	26	34
37	48	51	59	63	67
72	79	81	86	90	97

Prime number
Has only 2 factors (1 and itself),
e.g. 17, 19
Composite number
Has more than 2 factors,
e.g. 12, 16

Complete the factor trees and write each number as a product of prime factors.

27 = 3 x _____ x _____

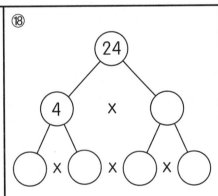

24 = _____

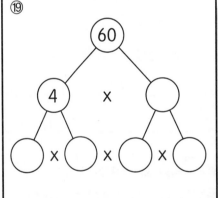

60 = _____

 **EXTRA Workout**

Solve the problems mentally.

⑳   5 x 18

= 5 x (10 + _____)

= 5 x 10 + 5 x _____

= _____ + _____

= _____

㉑   6 x 49

= 6 x (50 – _____)

= 6 x _____ – 6 x _____

= _____ – _____

= _____

Reminder

Use brackets to help solve the problems,
e.g. 4 x 13 = 4 x (10 + 3)
= 4 x 10 + 4 x 3
= 40 + 12
= 52

5

3 Decimals

Workout 1

Write the decimal number shown on each abacus in numerals and in words.
' . ' represents the decimal point.

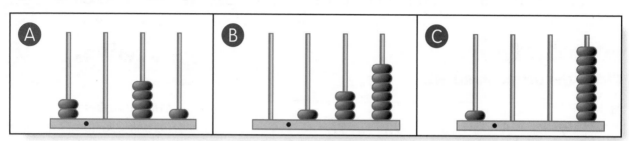

①   Ⓐ In numerals _____   In words _____

     Ⓑ In numerals _____   In words _____

     Ⓒ In numerals _____   In words _____

Fill in the missing numbers.

②   7.429   = 7 + _____ + 0.02 + _____

③   82.503 = 80 + 2 + _____ + _____

④   _____ = 30 + 0.06 + 0.005

⑤   _____ = 4 + 0.1 + 0.008

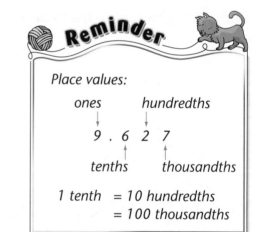

Reminder

Place values:

ones   hundredths
↓   ↓
9 . 6 2 7
   ↑   ↑
tenths   thousandths

1 tenth   = 10 hundredths
           = 100 thousandths

Workout 2

Write the correct numbers.

⑥   8 tenths   = _____ hundredths   = _____ thousandths

⑦   50 hundredths   = _____ tenths   = _____ thousandths

⑧   432 thousandths = _____ tenths _____ hundredths _____ thousandths

Do the multiplication or division mentally.

⑨   0.237 x 1000 = _____   ⑩   12.9 ÷ 100   = _____

⑪   3.65 x 0.1   = _____   ⑫   4.7 x 0.01   = _____

⑬   6 x 0.001   = _____   ⑭   0.073 x 1000 = _____

⑮   8.4 ÷ 100   = _____   ⑯   0.005 x 1000 = _____

Workout 3

Calculate.

⑰   6.093 + 5.168 = _____   ⑱   12.708 − 9.691 = _____

⑲   7.148 × 6   = _____   ⑳   0.315 ÷ 9   = _____

㉑   9.102 − 7.654 = _____   ㉒   5.907 × 8   = _____

㉓   2.472 ÷ 8   = _____   ㉔   4.009 + 7.892 = _____

Mom went shopping with her friends. Look at the prices and complete ㉕ to ㉚.

CHICKEN BURGERS 1.12 kg 8 pcs	ICE CREAM 2 L	JUICE 0.355 L	2 kg	TURKEY BREAST 6 slices 0.1 kg
$9.99	$3.49	$0.99	$2.14	$2.04

㉕   The average weight of 1 piece of chicken burger is _____ kg.

㉖   Mom bought 6 boxes of burgers. She bought _____ kg of burgers and needed to pay $ _____ .

㉗   Ms. Johnson bought 8 L of ice cream. She had to pay $ _____ .

㉘   8 cans of orange juice is _____ L. The total cost is $ _____ .

㉙   1 kg of strawberries costs $ _____ . Ms. White needed to pay $ _____ for 7 boxes of strawberries.

㉚   Ms. Goldman needed 48 slices of turkey breast. She had to buy _____ kg of turkey breast for $ _____ .

EXTRA Workout

Find how many cans of orange juice Ms. Lee bought.

㉛

> *I pay with a $50 bill for 3 boxes of chicken burgers, 6 kg of strawberries, 1 box of ice cream, and several cans of orange juice. I get a change of $0.22.*

She bought _____ cans of orange juice.

④ Rate and Ratio

Workout 1

Calculate the rates.

① | Run 200 km in 4 h | km/h |

② | Swim 105 m in 3 min | m/min |

③ | 12 L for 8 jars | L/jar |

④ | 51 kg for 6 bags | kg/bag |

Find the unit prices of the following items.

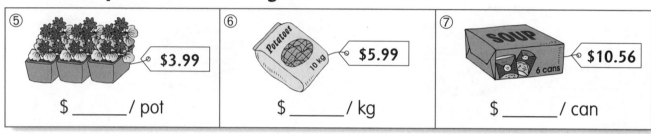

⑤ $3.99 $ _____ / pot

⑥ Potatoes 10 kg $5.99 $ _____ / kg

⑦ SOUP 6 cans $10.56 $ _____ / can

Workout 2

Write each ratio in two other ways.

⑧ $\frac{7}{9}$ _____ _____

⑨ 3 : 4 _____ _____

⑩ 15 to 8 _____ _____

> **Reminder**
>
> A ratio can be expressed in different ways:
> $$2 : 5, \frac{2}{5}, \text{ or } 2 \text{ to } 5$$
> Equivalent ratios:
>
> ⌐── x 5 ──┐
> 2 : 5 = 10 : 25
> ratio in   └── x 5 ──┘
> lowest terms

Write the equivalent ratios.

⑪ 6 : 5 = _____   ⑫ 12 : 9 = _____   ⑬ 7 : 8 = _____

⑭ 3 : 1 = _____   ⑮ 8 : 15 = _____   ⑯ 4 : 13 = _____

Write each ratio in lowest terms.

⑰ 6 : 18 _____   ⑱ 24 : 8 _____   ⑲ 15 : 3 _____

⑳ 10 to 14 _____   ㉑ 12 to 36 _____   ㉒ 12 to 16 _____

Look at the shapes. Write each ratio in lowest terms.

㉓ ★ : ♥ = _____   ㉔ ♥ : ★ = _____

㉕ ★ : Shapes = _____   ㉖ Shapes : ♥ = _____

Workout 3

Help mom find the unit price of each item sold in different stores. Then decide which store offers the best buy.

	Store A	Store B	Store C	Best buy
㉗ Tissue	8 rolls for $2.32 $ _____ / roll	4 rolls for $1.24 $ _____ / roll	6 rolls for $1.68 $ _____ /roll	Store _____
㉘ Juice	6 boxes for $1.74 $ _____ / box	3 boxes for $0.84 $ _____ / box	9 boxes for $2.70 $ _____ / box	Store _____
㉙ Film 100	3 rolls for $9.87 $ _____ / roll	8 rolls for $27.76 $ _____ / roll	2 rolls for $7.08 $ _____ / roll	Store _____

Complete the table to see how much water is needed to dilute different amounts of concentrated orange juice. Then complete the sentences.

㉚

Concentrated orange juice (can)	1	2	3	4	5	6
Water (can)	3					

㉛ The ratio of concentrated orange juice to water in lowest terms is _____ .

㉜ _____ cans of diluted orange juice can be made by mixing 2 cans of concentrated orange juice with water.

㉝ The ratio of concentrated orange juice to diluted orange juice in lowest terms is _____ .

EXTRA Workout

Ivan took 2 years to collect 128 stamps. Karen took 3 years to collect 168 stamps.

㉞ What is the ratio of Ivan's collection to Karen's in lowest terms? _____

㉟ Who collected the stamps at a faster rate? _____

㊱ Who will have a larger collection after 6 more years if they continue to collect the stamps at these rates? By how many more? _____

5 Percent

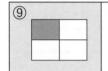

Rewrite each of the following using %.

> Percent (%) means a part of 100. Two percent, 2%, 2 out of 100, and $\frac{2}{100}$ are the same.

① Fifty-eight percent = _____

② Two hundred percent = _____

③ 82 out of 100 = _____   ④ 7 out of 100 = _____

⑤ $\frac{75}{100}$ = _____   ⑥ $\frac{36}{100}$ = _____   ⑦ $\frac{9}{100}$ = _____   ⑧ $\frac{104}{100}$ = _____

Estimate what percent of each shape is shaded.

⑨ ___ %   ⑩ ___ %   ⑪ ___ %   ⑫ ___ %

Rewrite the percents as fractions in lowest terms.

⑬ 48% = _____   ⑭ 5% = _____   ⑮ 125% = _____

⑯ 21% = _____   ⑰ 72% = _____   ⑱ 55% = _____

Rewrite the fractions with 100 as the denominator. Then write them as %.

⑲ $\frac{3}{4}$ = $\frac{}{100}$ = _____ %   ⑳ $\frac{2}{5}$ = _____ = _____ %

㉑ $\frac{7}{20}$ = _____ = _____ %   ㉒ $\frac{16}{25}$ = _____ = _____ %

Fill in the missing numerators. Then find the amount.

㉓ 22% = $\frac{22}{100}$ = $\frac{}{400}$

22% of 400 is _____ .

㉔ 60% = $\frac{60}{100}$ = $\frac{}{50}$

60% of 50 is _____ .

㉕ 45% = $\frac{}{100}$ = $\frac{}{20}$

45% of 20 is _____ .

㉖ 18% = $\frac{}{100}$ = $\frac{}{300}$

18% of 300 is _____ .

10

Workout 3

Look at the tally sheet made by Uncle Joe about his movie collection. Complete the table.

㉗

	Adventure	Comedy	Drama
No. of movies			
Percent of collection			

Adventure	Comedy	Drama

Ivan bought a bag of 50 balloons in 4 different colours. Complete the table and answer the question.

㉘

Colour	Red	Blue	Green	Yellow
Percent of the whole	32%	24%	16%	
No. of balloons				

㉙ Ivan inflated 50% of the red balloons and 75% of the blue balloons.
Which balloons did he inflate more? _____

EXTRA Workout

There are 25 children in Mr. Lowe's class. Complete the table and answer the questions.

	Boy	Girl	Total
㉚ No. of children with curly hair		9	12
Percent of the class			
㉛ No. of children with fair hair			
Percent of the class		28%	56%

㉜ What percent of children with curly hair are girls? _____

㉝ What percent of children with fair hair are boys? _____

㉞ 50% of curly-haired children are with fair hair. What % of children in the class are curly- and fair-haired? _____

11

⑥ Fractions

Workout 1

Write a fraction in lowest terms, a decimal and a percent to describe the shaded parts in each diagram.

	Fraction	Decimal	Percent
A			
B			
C			

① ② ③

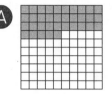

A

B

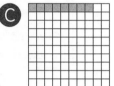

C

Change the improper fractions to mixed numbers.

④ $\dfrac{7}{5}$ = _____

⑤ $\dfrac{11}{8}$ = _____

⑥ $\dfrac{5}{4}$ = _____

⑦ $\dfrac{13}{9}$ = _____

Change the mixed numbers to improper fractions.

⑧ $2\dfrac{3}{4}$ = _____

⑨ $3\dfrac{1}{6}$ = _____

⑩ $1\dfrac{2}{3}$ = _____

⑪ $4\dfrac{5}{7}$ = _____

> ### Reminder
>
> Converting an improper fraction to a mixed number:
>
> $$\frac{5}{3} = 1\frac{2}{3} \qquad 3\overline{)5} \\ \underline{3} \\ 2$$
>
> Converting a mixed number to an improper fraction:
>
> $$1\frac{2}{3} = \frac{5}{3} \quad \begin{array}{l} \leftarrow 1 \times 3 + 2 = 5 \\ \leftarrow \text{remains the same} \end{array}$$

Workout 2

Compare the fractions, put > or < in the circles.

⑫ $3\dfrac{1}{2} \bigcirc \dfrac{11}{4}$

⑬ $2\dfrac{3}{10} \bigcirc \dfrac{14}{5}$

⑭ $\dfrac{13}{8} \bigcirc \dfrac{11}{6}$

⑮ $\dfrac{9}{4} \bigcirc \dfrac{13}{6}$

Put the fractions in order from least to greatest.

⑯ $1\dfrac{1}{2} \quad \dfrac{5}{3} \quad \dfrac{7}{4}$

⑰ $\dfrac{22}{9} \quad \dfrac{7}{3} \quad 2\dfrac{5}{6}$

_____ _____

> ### Reminder
>
> Comparing fractions:
> 1st Change improper fractions to mixed numbers.
> 2nd Compare the whole number part. If they are the same, go to the 3rd step.
> 3rd Compare the fraction part. Find their equivalent fractions with like denominator; then compare the numerators.

Workout 3

Write fractions to complete the addition or subtraction sentences.

⑱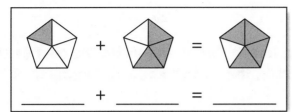

_____ + _____ = _____

⑲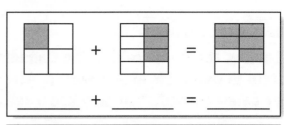

_____ + _____ = _____

⑳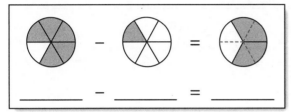

_____ − _____ = _____

㉑

_____ − _____ = _____

Add or subtract. Write the answers in lowest terms.

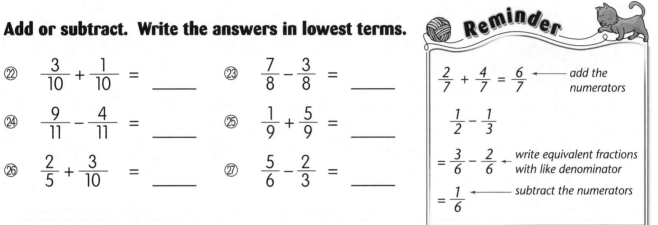

㉒ $\dfrac{3}{10} + \dfrac{1}{10} =$ _____

㉓ $\dfrac{7}{8} - \dfrac{3}{8} =$ _____

㉔ $\dfrac{9}{11} - \dfrac{4}{11} =$ _____

㉕ $\dfrac{1}{9} + \dfrac{5}{9} =$ _____

㉖ $\dfrac{2}{5} + \dfrac{3}{10} =$ _____

㉗ $\dfrac{5}{6} - \dfrac{2}{3} =$ _____

Reminder

$\dfrac{2}{7} + \dfrac{4}{7} = \dfrac{6}{7}$ ← add the numerators

$\dfrac{1}{2} - \dfrac{1}{3}$

$= \dfrac{3}{6} - \dfrac{2}{6}$ ← write equivalent fractions with like denominator

$= \dfrac{1}{6}$ ← subtract the numerators

EXTRA Workout

Karen is making a cake. Help her fill in the fractions.

㉘ Karen needs $\dfrac{1}{4}$ cup of butter for the frosting and $\dfrac{1}{2}$ cup of butter for the cake. She needs _____ cup of butter in all.

㉙ The recipe calls for $\dfrac{2}{5}$ cup of sugar and $\dfrac{3}{4}$ cup of flour. She needs _____ more cup of flour than sugar.

㉚ Karen has to pre-heat the oven for $\dfrac{1}{3}$ h and bake the cake for $\dfrac{1}{2}$ h. She has to turn on the oven for _____ h in all.

㉛ Karen eats $\dfrac{1}{8}$ of the cake and Ivan eats $\dfrac{1}{6}$ of the cake. Karen eats _____ less cake than Ivan.

㉜ They have eaten _____ of the cake altogether, and _____ of the cake is left.

Money

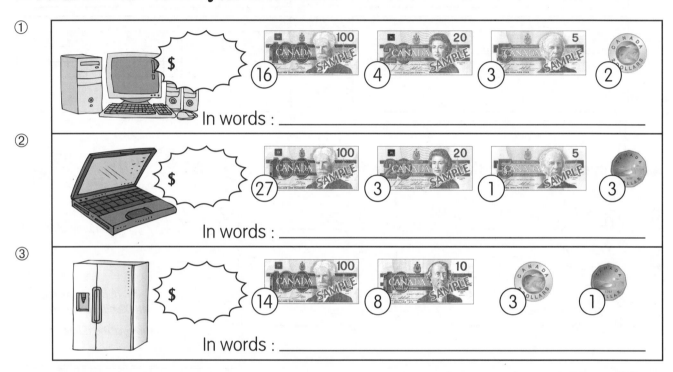

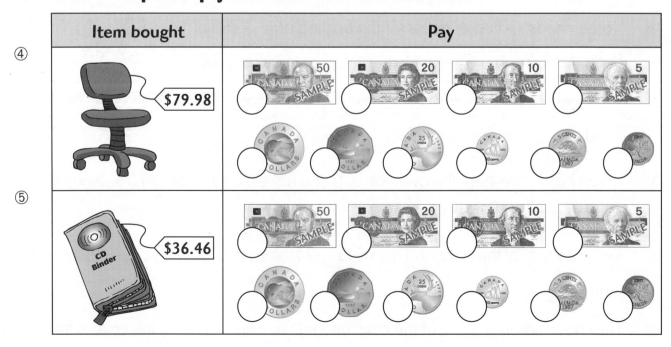

Look at the items sold at the Canadian MegaStore. Count and write the cost of each item in numerals and in words. The numbers in the circles show the number of bills or coins needed. You may use a calculator.

① In words : _____

② In words : _____

③ In words : _____

The children are shopping at the Canadian MegaStore. Fill in the correct numbers in the circles to help them pay with the fewest coins and bills.

Item bought	Pay
④ $79.98	
⑤ CD Binder $36.46	

14

Workout 2

After shopping, the children have some snacks in a restaurant. Look at the price list. Then complete the receipts.

⑥ **Uncle Joe's Restaurant**

Tuna sandwich $ _____

Fries $ _____

Milk $ _____

Subtotal $ _____

Amount reduced $ _____

Total due $ _____

Cash $ 8.15

Change $ _____

⑦ **Uncle Joe's Restaurant**

Hamburger $ _____

Fries $ _____

Orange Juice $ _____

Subtotal $ _____

Amount reduced $ _____

Total due $ _____

Cash $ 10.00

Change $ _____

Uncle Joe's Restaurant

Taxes included

Tuna sandwich	$3.40
Hamburger	$2.80
Fries	$1.25
Orange juice	$0.95
Milk	$0.75

For purchase of 5.00 or above, you can get 5¢ off each dollar.

EXTRA Workout

Some items at the Canadian MegaStore are on sale. Help the staff find the amount off each item and the sale price.

Reminder

$20   30% off

$$\frac{30}{100} = \frac{6}{20}; \text{ amount off is } \$6.$$
Sale price: $20 − $6 = $14

Canadian MegaStore

On Sale

		Percent Off	Amount Off	Sale Price
⑧	$25	25%	$	$
⑨	$20	15%	$	$
⑩	$120	20%	$	$
⑪	$18	30%	$	$

⑧ Time, Distance and Speed

Workout 1

Write the 24-hour clock times.

	12-h clock time	24-h clock time
	8:15:30 a.m.	08:15:30
	8:15:30 p.m.	20:15:30
	12:10:05 a.m.	00:10:05

Reminder

① [11:27:41 PM]   ② [02:16:35 AM]

③

A _____

B _____

C _____

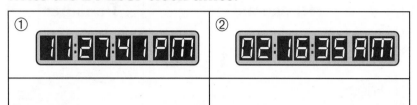

A   B   C

Write the times using a.m. or p.m.

④ 11:22:06 _____   ⑤ 03:17:25 _____

⑥ 18:07:52 _____   ⑦ 22:37:43 _____

Workout 2

Write the times using 24-h clock times.

⑧ 30 min after 4:40:15 p.m. _____

⑨ 1 h 45 min before 10:35:07 _____

⑩ 42 min 28 s before 03:47:10 _____

Reminder

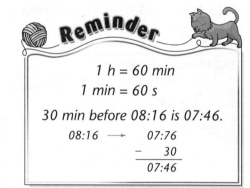

1 h = 60 min
1 min = 60 s

30 min before 08:16 is 07:46.

08:16 → 07:76
      −   30
         07:46

Fill in the blanks.

⑪ Karen started watching T.V. at 16:30 and finished at 18:05. She had been watching T.V. for _____ h _____ min.

⑫ It takes 18 min to drive from Karen's home to the cinema. If the movie starts at 16:30 and Karen has to be at the cinema 10 min before the show, the latest time she has to leave home is _____ : _____ .

⑬ Joe started to run a Marathon at 09:15:35 and finished at 13:20:55. He ran for _____ h _____ min _____ s.

16

Workout 3

The long-distance runners are practising for a competition. Look at the coach's record and fill in the missing data.

	Distance	Time	Speed
⑭	24 km	2 h	
⑮		3 h	11 km/h
⑯	5 km	$\frac{1}{2}$ h	
⑰	20 km		10 km/h
⑱		4 h	11.5 km/h
⑲	36 km		12 km/h

Reminder

Distance = Speed x Time
Speed = Distance ÷ Time
Time = Distance ÷ Speed

The children are cycling in a park. Help them solve the problems.

⑳ Ivan cycles 21 km in 2 h. What is his speed? _____ km/h

㉑ How far can Karen cover in half an hour at a speed of 11 km/h? _____ km

㉒ How long does Paul take to cycle 18 km at a speed of 10 km/h? _____ h

㉓ Stan cycles at a speed 0.5 km/h faster than that of Ted. How many more km can Stan cycle than Ted in 2 h? _____ km

Extra Workout

A police officer is monitoring speed on a highway. Help him solve the problems. You may use a calculator to do the multiplication.

㉔ A driver is found to be travelling 90 m in 2 s. His speed is _____ m/s.

㉕ Driving at this speed, the driver will travel _____ m in 100 s.

㉖ In 1 h (or 3600 s), the driver will travel _____ m.

㉗ The speed of this driver is _____ km/h.

⑨ Perimeter and Area

Write number sentences using mixed operations. Then calculate the perimeters.

① 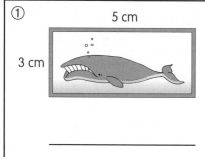 5 cm / 3 cm _____ = _____ cm	② 6 m _____ = _____ m	③ 5 dm / 4 dm 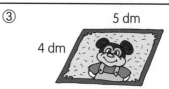 _____ = _____ dm
④ 8 cm 8 cm 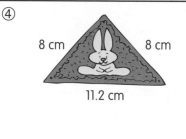 11.2 cm _____ = _____ cm	⑤ 5 m 7 m 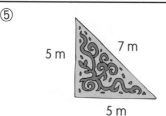 5 m _____ = _____ m	⑥ 4 dm 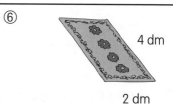 2 dm _____ = _____ dm

Calculate the area of each shape.

⑦ 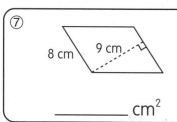 8 cm   9 cm

_____ cm²

⑧ 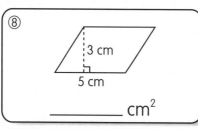 3 cm / 5 cm

_____ cm²

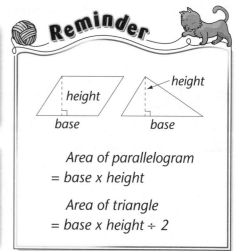

height / base   height / base

Area of parallelogram
= base x height

Area of triangle
= base x height ÷ 2

⑨ 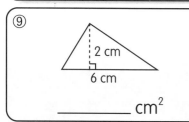 2 cm / 6 cm

_____ cm²

⑩ 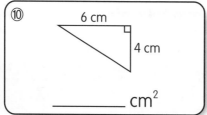 6 cm / 4 cm

_____ cm²

Look at the measures of the photo frame. Find the answers.

⑪   The area of the frame is _____ cm².

⑫   The perimeter of the frame is _____ cm.

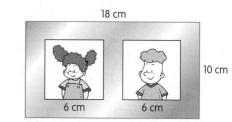

18 cm

10 cm

6 cm   6 cm

Workout 2

Draw the shapes. Colour the shape that has the greatest perimeter in each group.

⑬   Draw 3 different parallelograms, each having an area of 8 cm².

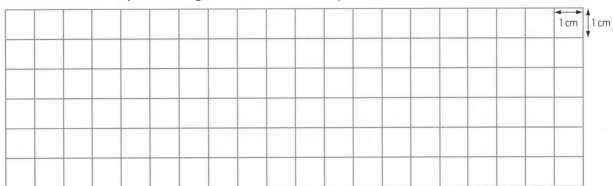

⑭   Draw an isosceles triangle, a right triangle, and a scalene triangle, each having an area of 6 cm².

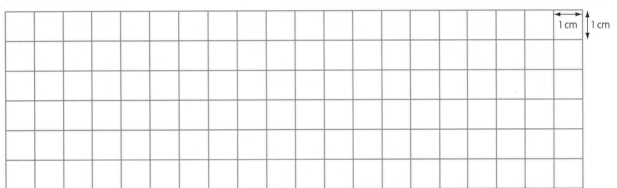

⑮   Draw a rectangle, a parallelogram, and a triangle, each having an area of 12 cm².

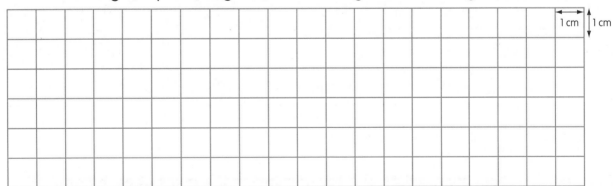

EXTRA Workout

Look at the kite made by Ivan. Solve the problem.

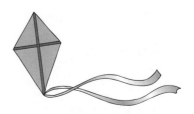

⑯   The framework of the kite is made with 2 thin sticks of lengths 30 cm and 45 cm. If the long stick cuts the short one in 2 equal lengths, what is the area of the kite?

_____ cm²

10 Volume and Mass

Workout 1

Calculate the volumes of the rectangular prisms.

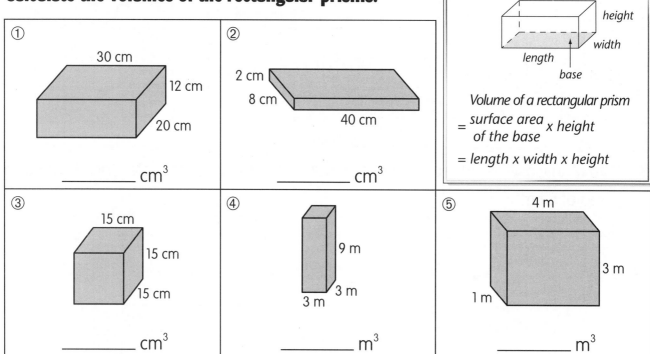

Reminder

Volume of a rectangular prism

$= \dfrac{\text{surface area}}{\text{of the base}} \times \text{height}$

$= \text{length} \times \text{width} \times \text{height}$

① 30 cm, 12 cm, 20 cm
_____ cm³

② 2 cm, 8 cm, 40 cm
_____ cm³

③ 15 cm, 15 cm, 15 cm
_____ cm³

④ 9 m, 3 m, 3 m
_____ m³

⑤ 4 m, 3 m, 1 m
_____ m³

Fill in the missing numbers in the table.

Surface area of the base (cm²)	⑥	82	251	176
Height (cm)	9	⑦	16	21
Volume (cm³)	1017	984	⑧	⑨

Workout 2

Check ✔ the most appropriate unit for measuring the mass of each item.

⑩ A feather   Ⓐ kilogram   Ⓑ gram   Ⓒ milligram

⑪ A bag of potatoes   Ⓐ kilogram   Ⓑ gram   Ⓒ milligram

⑫ A baseball   Ⓐ kilogram   Ⓑ gram   Ⓒ milligram

⑬ An exercise book   Ⓐ kilogram   Ⓑ gram   Ⓒ milligram

⑭ A paper clip   Ⓐ kilogram   Ⓑ gram   Ⓒ milligram

⑮ A baby   Ⓐ kilogram   Ⓑ gram   Ⓒ milligram

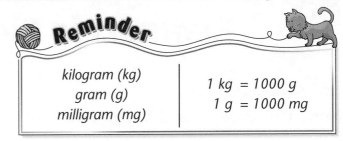

Fill in the missing numbers.

⑯ 7 g   = _____ mg

⑰ 2300 mg = _____ g

⑱ 1.8 kg   = _____ g

⑲ 5460 g   = _____ kg   ⑳ _____ kg = 304 g

㉑ 0.76 g   = _____ mg   ㉒ _____ g = 412 mg

Reminder

kilogram (kg) gram (g) milligram (mg)	1 kg = 1000 g 1 g = 1000 mg

Workout 3

Which is the better deal? Check ✔ the representing letter.

㉓

Ⓐ $1.20 / 0.1 kg

Ⓑ $2.56 / 200 g

㉔

Ⓐ 2¢ / 0.1 g

Ⓑ 9¢ / 500 mg

Each chocolate bean weighs 300 mg. Find the masses of the different packages.

㉕ Merry 180 pcs Tin : 25 g Mass : _____ g	㉖ Merry 250 pcs Box : 20 g Mass : _____ g	㉗ Merry 80 pcs Bag : 8 g Mass : _____ g

EXTRA Workout

Karen has a set of 6 books. Help her solve the problems.

㉘ What is the volume of each book?   _____ cm³

㉙ Each book weighs 450 g. The box holding the set of books weighs 550 g. What is the mass of the whole set of books including the box?   _____ kg

㉚ The box holding the books is made of cardboard of thickness 2 mm. What is the volume of the box? Use a calculator to help get the answer.   _____ cm³

1 cm
24 cm
16 cm

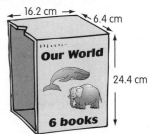

16.2 cm
6.4 cm
24.4 cm
Our World
6 books

11 Geometric Figures

Workout 1

Write the name of the 3-D figure that can be made from each net.

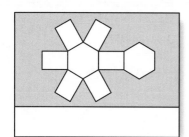
①

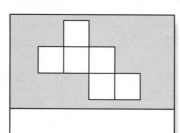
②

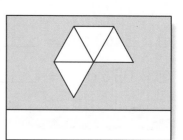
③

Look at the following 3-D figures. Sketch the nets on the grids.

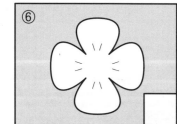
④

⑤

Reminder

This figure fits on itself 4 times in a full turn. It has rotational symmetry of order 4.

turn centre

Workout 2

Draw all the lines of symmetry of each shape and write the order of symmetry in the box.

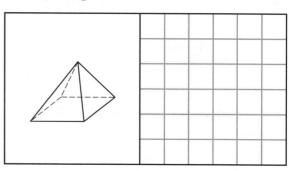
⑥ ⑦ ⑧ ⑨

Colour the figures similar to the shaded shape blue and the congruent figures green.

⑩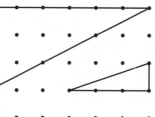

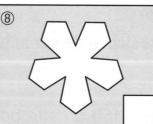

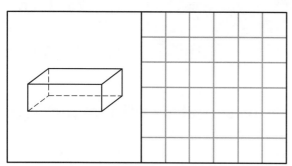

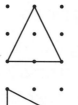

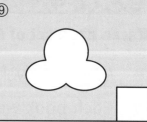

Measure the angles. Then name the triangles by writing 'Acute-angled', 'Right', or 'Obtuse-angled'.

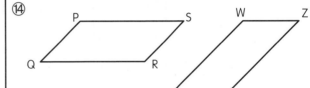

⑪

Number of angles				
	Right			
	Acute			
	Obtuse			
⑫	Name of triangle			

EXTRA Workout

Measure the angles and sides of each pair of congruent shapes. Then match the corresponding angles and sides.

⑬

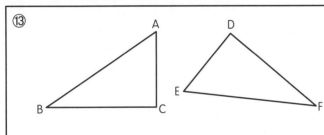

∠ A = ∠ E   AB = EF

∠ B = ∠ _____   AC = _____

∠ C = ∠ _____   BC = _____

⑭

∠ P = ∠ _____   PQ = _____

∠ Q = ∠ _____   PS = _____

∠ R = ∠ _____   QR = _____

∠ S = ∠ _____   SR = _____

Draw the shapes.

⑮ Construct 2 angles, 50° and 130°, one at either end of the given line, both with the other arm equal to 3 cm. Then make a parallelogram.

_____

⑯ Complete the figure so that it has 2 lines of symmetry. Draw all the lines of symmetry.

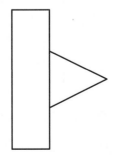

Transformations and Coordinates

Workout 1

Draw the transformed images and write the coordinates.

① Reflect A over ℓ. Label the image B. Then rotate B $\frac{1}{2}$ turn about P. Label the image C.

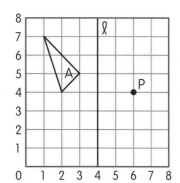

Coordinates of the three vertices of C:

_____

② Rotate T $\frac{1}{4}$ turn clockwise about Q. Label the image R. Then translate R 1 unit right and 2 units down. Label the image S.

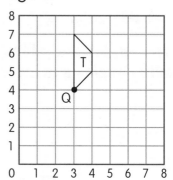

Coordinates of the four vertices of S:

_____

Draw the transformed images and describe the transformations.

③ Reflect L over ℓ_1. Label the image M. Then reflect M over ℓ_2. Label the image N.

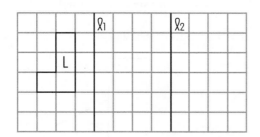

A single transformation to move L onto N: _____

④ Rotate G $\frac{3}{4}$ turn clockwise about P. Label the image F. Then reflect F over ℓ_3. Label the image H.

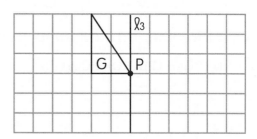

A single transformation to move G onto H: _____

Workout 2

Complete the tiling pattern and describe the transformations.

⑤   a.

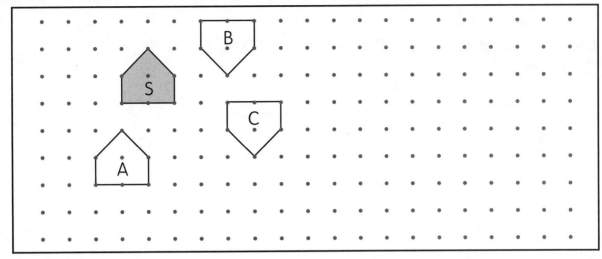

b.   Move S onto A : _____

c.   Move S onto B : _____

d.   Move S onto C : _____

EXTRA Workout

Locate the images and check ✔ the correct transformations to get the images. Then describe the transformations as specified.

Translation	Direction and distance of the move
Reflection	Draw the line of reflection
Rotation	The coordinates of the centre of rotation and the amount of rotation

⑥   a.   Join (2,1), (4,3), (6,2), (4,0), and (2,1) to get the image of A.

b.   Ⓐ Translation   Ⓑ Reflection   Ⓒ Rotation

_____

⑦   a.   Join (4,4), (6,4), (6,3), (4,1), (4,2), (5,3), (4,3), and (4,4) to get the image of B.

b.   Ⓐ Translation   Ⓑ Reflection   Ⓒ Rotation

_____

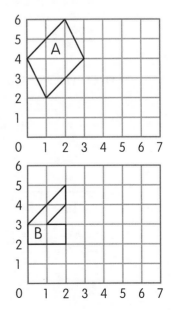

13 Patterns

Workout 1

Look for the patterns. Describe the rules and extend the patterns.

①   1   3   7   15   31   ____   ____   ____

     Rule _____

②   1   4   10   22   46   ____   ____   ____

     Rule _____

③   3   4   6   10   18   ____   ____   ____

     Rule _____

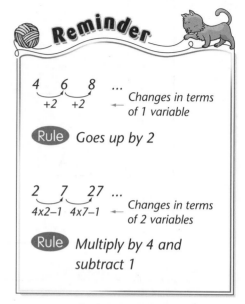

Reminder

4   6   8 ...   ← Changes in terms of 1 variable
   +2   +2

Rule *Goes up by 2*

2   7   27 ...   ← Changes in terms of 2 variables
4x2–1   4x7–1

Rule *Multiply by 4 and subtract 1*

The children are making models. Look for the patterns and draw 2 more pictures. Then complete the charts and write the rules that relate the 2 numbers in each column.

④   Ivan adds triangles made of toothpicks to extend the pattern.

    a.

b.

No. of triangles	1	2	3	4	5	6
No. of toothpicks	3	5				

c.   Rule _____

⑤   Karen adds squares and triangles to extend the pattern.

    a.

b.

No. of squares	1	2	3	4	5	6
No. of triangles	3					

c.   Rule _____

26

Workout 2

The girls are making bracelets with beads in different colours. Graph the relationships and state the rules that relate the number of beads in different colours.

⑥ a.

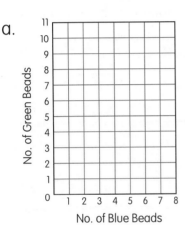

No. of Red Beads
No. of Blue Beads

No. of blue beads	1	2	3	4	5
No. of red beads	2	4	6	8	10

b. No. of red beads _____
_____ the no. of blue beads.

⑦ a.

No. of Green Beads
No. of Blue Beads

No. of blue beads	1	2	3	4	5
No. of green beads	3	5	7	9	11

b. No. of green beads _____
_____

EXTRA Workout

Stan is saving for a toy car. The amount of tax paid when buying things follows a pattern. Complete the graph to show the pattern and answer the questions.

⑧

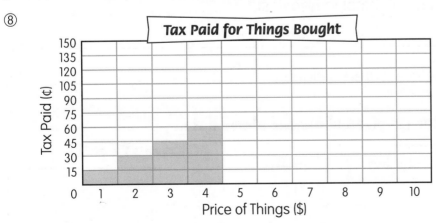

Tax Paid for Things Bought

Tax Paid (¢)
Price of Things ($)

$25

⑨ What is the pattern of tax paid?

_____

⑩ How much does Stan need to save for the toy car? $ _____

14 Data Management

Nurse Nancy measures the weights of 12 children. Use her records to complete the scatter plot and answer the questions.

Age (year)	9	10	11	12
Weight (kg)	36, 37	36, 38, 39	38, 39, 40, 41	39, 40, 42

①

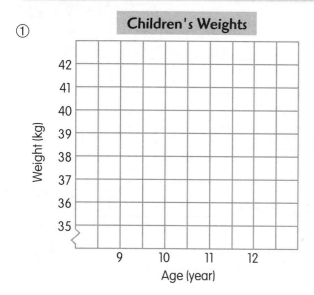

Children's Weights

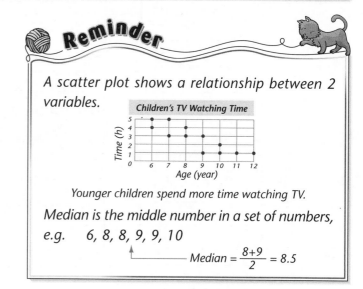

Reminder

A scatter plot shows a relationship between 2 variables.

Children's TV Watching Time

Younger children spend more time watching TV.

Median is the middle number in a set of numbers, e.g.   6, 8, 8, 9, 9, 10

$$Median = \frac{8+9}{2} = 8.5$$

② What is the relationship between the ages and the weights of the children shown in the scatter plot?

_____

③ Put the weights in order from lightest to heaviest.

_____

④ What is the median of the measured weights?   _____ kg

Complete the table and the bar graph to show the above data.

⑤

Weight (kg)	No. of children
36 – 37	
38 – 39	
40 – 41	
42 and above	

⑥

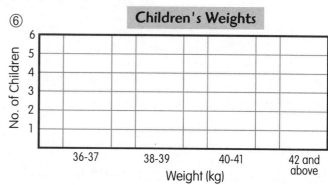

Children's Weights

28

Workout 2

Nurse Nancy uses a line graph to keep records of the weights of 2 babies, Sean and Amy. Use the graph to answer the questions.

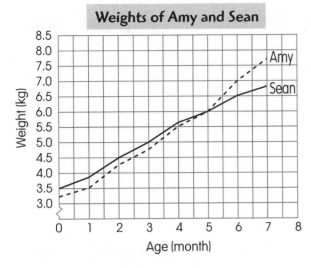

⑦ Who was heavier at new born?

_____

⑧ What was the weight of Sean at 3 months?

_____ kg

⑨ What was the weight of Amy at 6 months?

_____ kg

⑩ How many months after birth did the babies have the same weight? What was the weight?

_____ months

_____ kg

⑪ How many months after birth did the babies have the greatest difference in weight? What was the difference in weight?

_____ months

_____ kg

⑫ Following the tendency of growth, estimate the weights of Sean and Amy at 8 months.

Sean : _____ kg

Amy : _____ kg

Extra Workout

Use the line graph above to answer the questions.

⑬ Which baby's weight increased more evenly? Explain.

_____

⑭ Are there any better graphs than the line graph for showing the increase in weight of the babies? Explain.

_____

_____

15 Probability

Workout 1

Fill in the correct numbers to indicate the possible events and the probabilities.

① **Toss a coin** : There are _____ possible events. The probability of having heads up is _____ .

② **Roll a dice** : There are _____ possible events. The probability of getting a 3 is _____ .

③ **Toss a paper cup** : There are _____ possible events. The probability of landing on its side is _____ .

④ **Toss a bottle cap** : There are _____ possible events. After landing on the open side in a toss, the probability of landing on the open side in the following toss is _____ .

Workout 2

Complete the tree diagram to show all possible events and write the probabilities in fractions in lowest terms.

When you toss a coin, you get either heads (H) or tails (T). When you roll a dice, you get 1, 2, 3, 4, 5, or 6.

⑤ Ivan tosses a coin and then rolls a numbered dice.

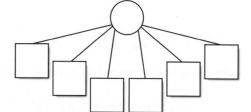

Toss a coin

Roll a dice

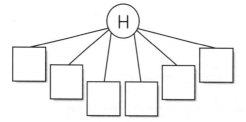

⑥ How many possible events are there? _____

⑦ What is the probability of each of the following particular events?

a. Head and 6 _____   b. Tail and 3 _____

c. Head and even number _____   d. Tail and a number greater than 4 _____

The Day family has 3 children. Complete the tree diagram to show the possible combinations. Then answer the questions.

⑧

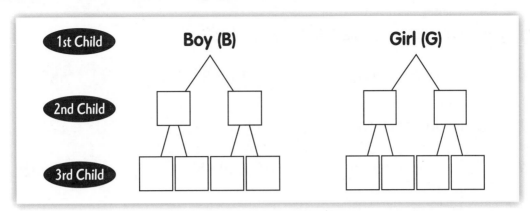

⑨ How many possible combinations are there? _____

⑩ What is the probability of each of the following?

a. 1 boy and 2 girls _____   b. At least 1 girl _____

c. 3 girls _____   d. At least 2 boys _____

e. 2nd child being a boy _____   f. 3rd child being a girl _____

⑪ Mr. Day says if his 3rd child is a boy, there will be a greater chance for the 4th child to be a girl. Is he correct? Explain.

_____

EXTRA Workout

Karen has a set of 6 number cards. She shuffles the cards each time and lets Ivan draw 1 card. Write the probabilities and predict the results.

⑫ What is the probability of drawing each number?

1 _____ **2** _____ **3** _____ **5** _____

A number greater than 5 _____

A number smaller than 6 _____

⑬ Ivan draws the cards 120 times. Predict the number of times that each number is drawn.

1 about _____ times   **2** about _____ times

3 about _____ times   **5** about _____ times

Check ✔ the letter which represents the correct answer in each problem.

① Which of the following equals 683 thousandths?

    Ⓐ 0.683   Ⓑ 6.83   Ⓒ 68.3   Ⓓ 683

② Which ratio is in lowest terms?

    Ⓐ 9 : 15   Ⓑ 3 : 5   Ⓒ 14 : 8   Ⓓ 21 : 35

③ 27% of $300 is $ _____ .

    Ⓐ 27   Ⓑ 30   Ⓒ 9   Ⓓ 81

④ $\frac{35}{8}$ converted to a mixed number is _____ .

    Ⓐ $3\frac{5}{8}$ Ⓑ $4\frac{5}{8}$ Ⓒ $4\frac{3}{8}$ Ⓓ $5\frac{3}{8}$

⑤ The probability of spinning a composite number is _____ .

    Ⓐ $\frac{3}{8}$ Ⓑ $\frac{1}{2}$ Ⓒ $\frac{5}{8}$ Ⓓ $\frac{3}{4}$

⑥ 1 h 25 min before 01:10:05 is _____ .

    Ⓐ 02:35:05   Ⓑ 00:45:55   Ⓒ 23:44:45   Ⓓ 23:45:05

⑦ A car travels 315 km from 11:30 to 14:30. Its speed is _____ km/h.

    Ⓐ 105   Ⓑ 157.5   Ⓒ 115   Ⓓ 78.75

⑧ The order of rotational symmetry of is _____ .

    Ⓐ 8   Ⓑ 2   Ⓒ 6   Ⓓ 4

⑨ Which net can make a cube?

    Ⓐ 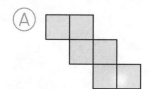   Ⓑ 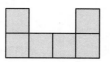   Ⓒ 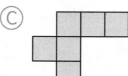   Ⓓ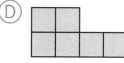

Do the calculation. Write fractions in lowest terms.

⑩	⑪	⑫	⑬
$\begin{array}{r}3\,2\,7\\ \times\quad4\,8\\\hline\end{array}$	$16\,\overline{)\,1\,5\,7\,3}$	$8\,\overline{)\,5.0\,8}$	$\begin{array}{r}2\,7\,3\\5\,1\,6\\4\,2\,9\\+\ 3\,8\,2\\\hline\end{array}$

⑭ 4.658×7 = _____

⑮ $3.076 + 5.809$ = _____

⑯ $9.006 - 3.65$ = _____

⑰ $11\,260 - 7963$ = _____

⑱ $96 - 54 \div 3 + 6$ = _____

⑲ $8 \times 12 + 76 \div 4$ = _____

⑳ $\dfrac{11}{12} - \dfrac{7}{12}$ = _____

㉑ $\dfrac{1}{4} + \dfrac{2}{3}$ = _____

Complete the table. Write fractions and ratios in lowest terms.

	Fraction	Decimal	Percent	Ratio
㉒	$\dfrac{3}{5}$			
㉓		0.45		
㉔			24%	
㉕				7 : 20

Write the first ten multiples of each number. Then find the least common multiple (L.C.M.) of each group of numbers.

		First 10 multiples	Common multiples	L.C.M.
㉖	6			
	8			
㉗	4			
	5			

List all the factors of each number. Then find the greatest common factor (G.C.F.) of each group of numbers.

㉘ 12 _____

㉙ 20 _____

㉚ 30 _____

㉛ 45 _____

㉜ G.C.F. of 12 and 20 _____

㉝ G.C.F. of 30 and 45 _____

㉞ G.C.F. of 12 and 30 _____

㉟ G.C.F. of 20 and 30 _____

Karen is preparing for her birthday party. Help her fill in the missing numbers.

㊱ She buys 3 bags of potato chips for $2.04. The price of 1 bag of chips is _____ ¢.

㊲ 5 jars of juice are made by mixing 2 jars of fruit punch with water. The ratio of fruit punch to water is _____ : _____ .

㊳ Karen invites 9 friends to her party. 4 of them are boys. _____ % of children at the party will be girls.

㊴ The party starts at 2:30 p.m. and ends at 18:00. The party lasts _____ h _____ min.

㊵ Ted lives at a distance of 2 km from Karen's house. He took 10 min to cycle to Karen's house at a speed of _____ km/h.

Look at Karen's birthday cake and help her solve the problems.

㊶ The box for the cake is a cube with side length 20 cm. What is the surface area of the base of the box? _____ cm^2

㊷ What is the perimeter of the base? _____ cm

㊸ What is the volume of the box? _____ cm^3

㊹ The mass of the cake is 900 g. Mom puts 11 candles each of mass 800 mg on the cake. What is the total mass of the cake with the candles? _____ g

㊺ The cake is cut into 12 slices. What is the mass of each slice? _____ g

Karen is making name plates. Help her complete the drawings to find out the shape of each plate and the picture to be drawn on it.

㊻ Construct 2 angles, each of 60°, one at either end of the given line, both with the other arm equal to 3 cm. Join the ends of the arms with a straight line.

_____

The shape is a _____ .

㊼ Complete the figure so that it has 4 lines of symmetry. Draw all the lines of symmetry.

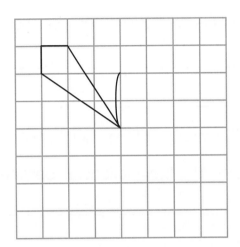

On the back of each name plate is a tiling pattern made with the shaded shape T. Complete the tiling pattern and describe the transformations in two different ways.

㊽

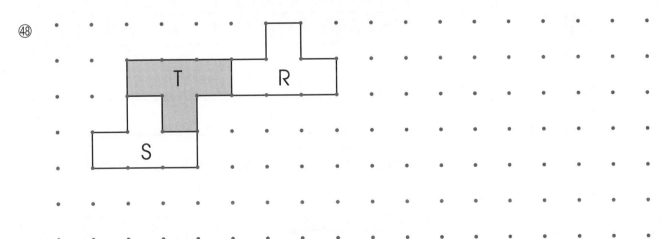

	a. With a single transformation	b. With more than one transformation
㊾ Move T onto R		
㊿ Move T onto S		

The children measured their heights and shoe sizes. Look at the records of their heights and the scatter plot, and answer the questions.

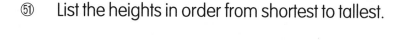

Height of children in cm				
155	162	166	160	154
154	160	158	161	157

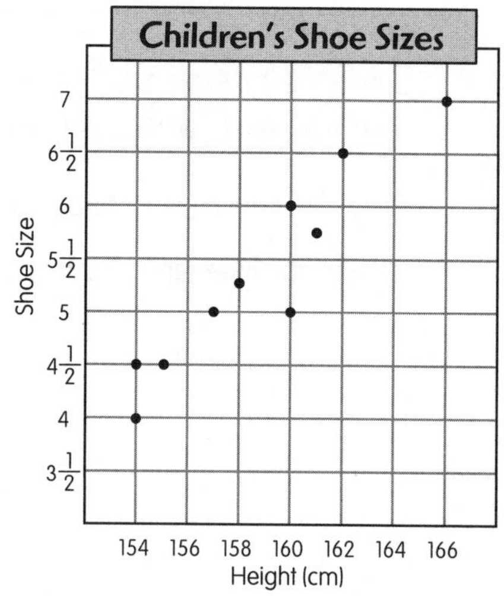

(51) List the heights in order from shortest to tallest.

____

____

(52) The median of their heights is ______ cm.

(53) Describe the relationship between the heights of the children and their shoe sizes.

____

Look how Karen has mixed the nuts. Graph the relationships, state the rules, and fill in the missing numbers.

(54) a.

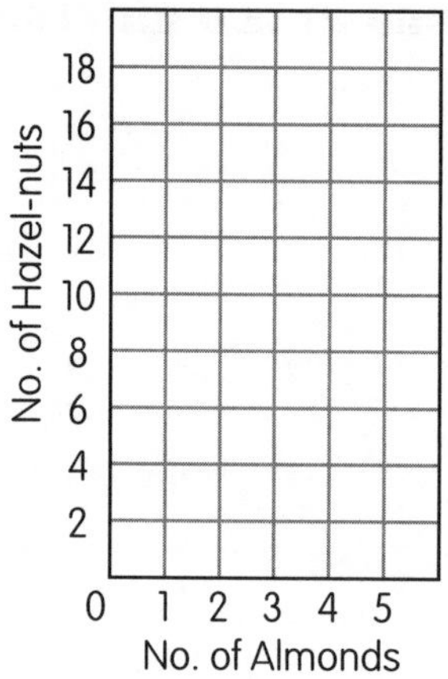

No. of almonds	1	2	3	4	5
No. of hazel-nuts	2	6	10	14	18

b. Rule : __________________________________

____

c. Karen adds _____ hazel-nuts for 8 almonds.

(55) a.

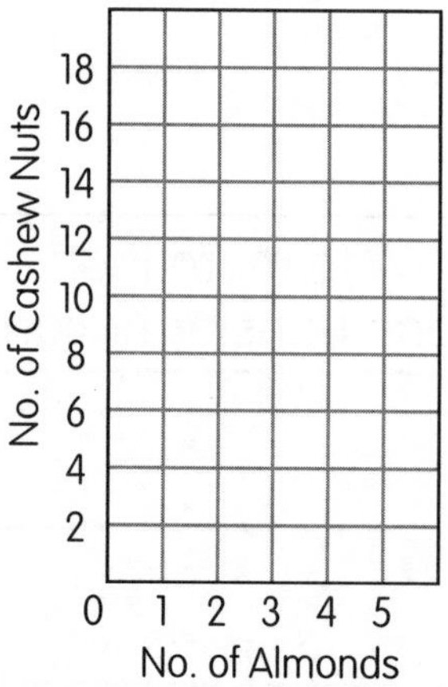

No. of almonds	1	2	3	4	5
No. of cashew nuts	5	8	11	14	17

b. Rule : __________________________________

____

c. Karen adds 29 cashew nuts for _____ almonds.

1   Operations with Whole Numbers

1. 1951

2.
```
        2 7 3
    x     4 6
    1 6 3 8
  1 0 9 2 0
  1 2 5 5 8
```

3.
```
         2 3
    19 ) 4 3 7
         3 8
           5 7
           5 7
```

4.
```
    )
```

5. 2025
6. 17 035
7. 6834
8. 1567
9. 21 252
10. 173
11. 87R20
12. 40 252
13. 22 065
14. 83 R58
15. 39
16. 17
17. 18
18. 54
19. 45
20. 44
21. 35
22. 36
23. 62
24. 58
25. 10
26. 44
27. 6
28. 1152 ÷ 16 = 72 ; 72
29. 552 x 18 = 9936 ; 9936
30. No. of non-big books: 300 – 48 = 252 ;
    No. of bookshelves: 252 ÷ 27 = 9R9 ; 10
31. No. of books on 7 shelves: 36 x 7 = 252 ;
    No. of books on 12 shelves: 828 – 252 = 576 ;
    No. of books on each bookshelf: 576 ÷ 12 = 48 ; 48
32. 2832
33. 236 ; 96 ; 46 ; 25 ; 69

2   Number Theory

1 - 4.
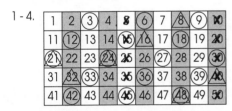

5. 6, 12, 18, 24, 30, 36, 42, 48 ; 6
6. 15, 30, 45 ; 15
7. 24, 48 ; 24
8. 18 ; 9 ; 6
9. 28 ; 14 ; 7
10. 36 ; 18 ; 12 ; 9 ; 6
11. 48 ; 24 ; 16 ; 12 ; 8
12. 1, 2, 3, 6, 9, 18 ;
    1, 2, 4, 7, 14, 28 ;
    1, 2, 3, 4, 6, 9, 12, 18, 36 ;
    1, 2, 3, 4, 6, 8, 12, 16, 24, 48
13. 1, 2, 4 ; 4
14. 1, 2, 3, 6 ; 6
15. 1, 2, 4 ; 4
16. 2, 5, 23, 37, 59, 67, 79, 97
17.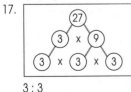
    3 ; 3
18.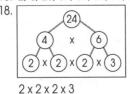
    2 x 2 x 2 x 3
19.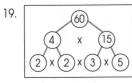
    2 x 2 x 3 x 5

20. 8 ; 8 ; 50 ; 40 ; 90
21. 1 ; 50 ; 1 ; 300 ; 6 ; 294

3   Decimals

1. A 2.041 ; 2 and 41 thousandths
   B 0.136 ; 136 thousandths
   C 1.008 ; 1 and 8 thousandths
2. 0.4 ; 0.009
3. 0.5 ; 0.003
4. 30.065
5. 4.108
6. 80 ; 800
7. 5 ; 500
8. 4 ; 3 ; 2
9. 237
10. 0.129
11. 0.365
12. 0.047
13. 0.006
14. 73
15. 0.084
16. 5
17. 11.261
18. 3.017
19. 42.888
20. 0.035
21. 1.448
22. 47.256
23. 0.309
24. 11.901
25. 0.14
26. 6.72 ; 59.94
27. 13.96
28. 2.84 ; 7.92
29. 1.07 ; 14.98
30. 0.8 ; 16.32
31. 10

4   Rate and Ratio

1. 50
2. 35
3. 1.5
4. 8.5
5. 1.33
6. 0.599
7. 1.76
8. 7 to 9 ; 7 : 9
9. 3 to 4 ; $\frac{3}{4}$
10. 15 : 8 ; $\frac{15}{8}$

11 - 16.   (Suggestedd answers)
11. 12 : 10
12. 4 : 3
13. 14 : 16
14. 9 : 3
15. 16 : 30
16. 12 : 39
17. 1 : 3
18. 3 : 1
19. 5 : 1
20. 5 to 7
21. 1 to 3
22. 3 to 4
23. 3 : 2
24. 2 : 3
25. 3 : 5
26. 5 : 2
27. 0.29 ; 0.31 ; 0.28 ; C
28. 0.29 ; 0.28 ; 0.30 ; B
29. 3.29 ; 3.47 ; 3.54 ; A
30. 6 ; 9 ; 12 ; 15 ; 18
31. 1 ; 3
32. 8
33. 1 : 4
34. 16 : 21
35. Ivan
36. Ivan ; 8 more

5   Percent

1. 58%
2. 200%
3. 82%
4. 7%
5. 75%
6. 36%
7. 9%
8. 104%
9. 25
10. 50
11. 75
12. 40
13. $\frac{12}{25}$
14. $\frac{1}{20}$
15. $\frac{5}{4}$ or $1\frac{1}{4}$
16. $\frac{21}{100}$
17. $\frac{18}{25}$
18. $\frac{11}{20}$
19. 75 ; 75
20. $\frac{40}{100}$; 40
21. $\frac{35}{100}$; 35
22. $\frac{64}{100}$; 64
23. 88 ; 88
24. 30 ; 30
25. 45 ; 9 ; 9
26. 18 ; 54 ; 54
27. 25 ; 42 ; 33 ; 25% ; 42% ; 33%
28. 28% ; 16 ; 12 ; 8 ; 14
29. Blue
30. 3 ; 12% ; 36% ; 48%
31. 7 ; 7 ; 14 ; 28%
32. 75%
33. 50%
34. 24%

6   Fractions

1. $\frac{7}{20}$; 0.35 ; 35%
2. $\frac{21}{25}$; 0.84 ; 84%
3. $\frac{2}{25}$; 0.08 ; 8%
4. $1\frac{2}{5}$
5. $1\frac{3}{8}$
6. $1\frac{1}{4}$
7. $1\frac{4}{9}$
8. $\frac{11}{4}$
9. $\frac{19}{6}$
10. $\frac{5}{3}$
11. $\frac{33}{7}$
12. >
13. <

14. <   15. >

16. $1\frac{1}{2}$, $\frac{5}{3}$, $\frac{7}{4}$ 17. $\frac{7}{3}$, $\frac{22}{9}$, $2\frac{5}{6}$

18. $\frac{1}{5}$; $\frac{3}{5}$; $\frac{4}{5}$ 19. $\frac{1}{4}$; $\frac{3}{8}$; $\frac{5}{8}$

20. $\frac{5}{6}$; $\frac{1}{6}$; $\frac{4}{6}$ or $\frac{2}{3}$ 21. $\frac{2}{3}$; $\frac{4}{9}$; $\frac{2}{9}$

22. $\frac{2}{5}$ 23. $\frac{1}{2}$ 24. $\frac{5}{11}$

25. $\frac{2}{3}$ 26. $\frac{7}{10}$ 27. $\frac{1}{6}$

28. $\frac{3}{4}$ 29. $\frac{7}{20}$ 30. $\frac{5}{6}$

31. $\frac{1}{24}$ 32. $\frac{7}{24}$; $\frac{17}{24}$

7 Money

1. 1699 ; One thousand six hundred ninety-nine dollars
2. 2768 ; Two thousand seven hundred sixty-eight dollars
3. 1487 ; One thousand four hundred eighty-seven dollars
4. 1 ; 1 ; 0 ; 1 ; 2 ; 0 ; 3 ; 2 ; 0 ; 3
5. 0 ; 1 ; 1 ; 1 ; 0 ; 1 ; 1 ; 2 ; 0 ; 1
6. 3.40 ; 1.25 ; 0.75 ; 5.40 ; 0.25 ; 5.15 ; 3.00
7. 2.80 ; 1.25 ; 0.95 ; 5.00 ; 0.25 ; 4.75 ; 5.25
8. 6.25 ; 18.75   9. 3.00 ; 17.00
10. 24.00 ; 96.00   11. 5.40 ; 12.60

8 Time, Distance and Speed

1. 23:27:41   2. 02:16:35
3. A 21:05 ; B 08:50 ; C 00:35:15
4. 11:22:06 a.m.   5. 3:17:25 a.m.   6. 6:07:52 p.m.
7. 10:37:43 p.m.   8. 17:10:15   9. 08:50:07
10. 03:04:42   11. 1 ; 35   12. 16 ; 02
13. 4 ; 5 ; 20   14. 12 km/h   15. 33 km
16. 10 km/h   17. 2 h   18. 46 km
19. 3 h   20. 10.5   21. 5.5
22. 1.8   23. 1   24. 45
25. 4500   26. 162 000   27. 162

9 Perimeter and Area

1. 5 x 2 + 3 x 2 ; 16   2. 6 x 4 ; 24
3. 5 x 2 + 4 x 2 ; 18   4. 8 x 2 + 11.2 ; 27.2
5. 5 x 2 + 7 ; 17   6. 4 x 2 + 2 x 2 ; 12
7. 72   8. 15   9. 6
10. 12   11. 108   12. 104
13 - 15. (Suggested drawings)

13.
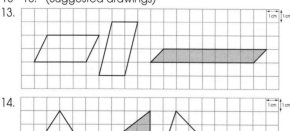

14.

15.

16. 675

10 Volume and Mass

1. 7200   2. 640   3. 3375
4. 81   5. 12   6. 113
7. 12   8. 4016   9. 3696
10. C   11. A   12. B
13. B   14. C   15. A
16. 7000   17. 2.3   18. 1800
19. 5.46   20. 0.304   21. 760
22. 0.412   23. A   24. B
25. 79   26. 95   27. 32
28. 384   29. 3.25   30. 2529.792

11 Geometric Figures

1. Hexagonal prism   2. Cube
3. Tetrahedron or Triangular pyramid
4 - 5. (Suggested drawings)

4.

5.
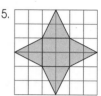

6.
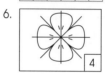

7.

8.
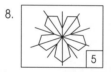

9.
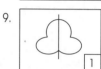

10. g = green   b = blue
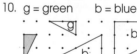

11. Right: 0 ; 1 ; 0   Acute: 3 ; 2 ; 2   Obtuse: 0 ; 0 ; 1
12. Acute-angled; Right; Obtuse-angled
13. F ; ED ; D ; FD
14. W (or Y) ; WZ (or YX) ; Z (or X) ; WX (or YZ) ; Y (or W) ; ZY (or XW) ; X (or Z) ; XY (or ZW)
15 -16. (Suggested drawings)

15.

16.
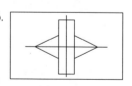

12 Transformations and Coordinates

1.
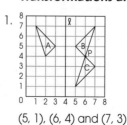

(5, 1), (6, 4) and (7, 3)

2.

(4, 2), (5, 1), (6, 1) and (7, 2)

3.

Translate L 8 units right

4.
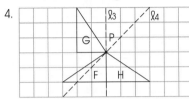

Reflect G over ℓ_4

5a.
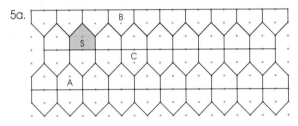

b - d. (Suggested answers)
b. Reflect S; then rotate the reflection image
c. Translate S; then rotate the translation image
d. Translate S; then reflect the translation image

6a.
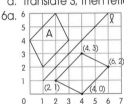
   b. B ; Reflect A over ℓ

7a.
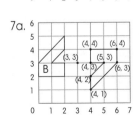
   b. C ; Rotate B $\frac{1}{2}$ turn about (3,3)

13 Patterns

1. 63 ; 127 ; 255 ; Multiply by 2 and add 1
2. 94 ; 190 ; 382 ; Add 1 and multiply by 2
3. 34 ; 66 ; 130 ; Subtract 1 and multiply by 2

4a.
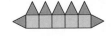

b. 7 ; 9 ; 11 ; 13
c. No. of triangles x 2 + 1 = No. of toothpicks

5a.

---

b. 4 ; 5 ; 6 ; 7 ; 8
c. No. of squares + 2 = No. of triangles

6a.
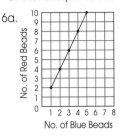
   b. equals 2 times

7a.
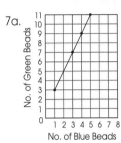
   b. equals 2 times the no. of blue beads plus 1.

8.
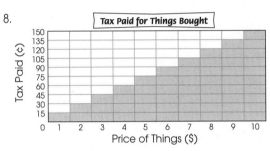

9. The amount of tax paid for every $1 is 15¢.
10. 28.75

14 Data Management

1.
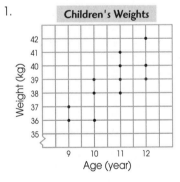

2. Generally, older children are heavier.
3. 36, 36, 37, 38, 38, 39, 39, 39, 40, 40, 41, 42
4. 39   5. 3 ; 5 ; 3 ; 1

6.
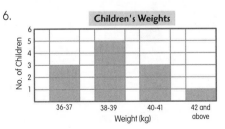

7. Sean   8. 5.0   9. 7.0
10. 5 ; 6.0   11. 7 ; 1.0
12 - 14. (Suggested answers)
12. 7.2 ; 8.5
13. Sean. His weight increased uniformly, but Amy's weight increased abruptly after 5 months.

14. No. Weight changes continuously, and the line graph is best for displaying continuously changing data.

15   Probability

1. $2 ; \dfrac{1}{2}$ 2. $6 ; \dfrac{1}{6}$

3. $3 ; \dfrac{3}{5}$ (Suggested answer)   4. $2 ; \dfrac{1}{2}$

5.

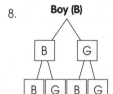 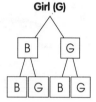

6. 12

7a. $\dfrac{1}{12}$ b. $\dfrac{1}{12}$ c. $\dfrac{1}{4}$ d. $\dfrac{1}{6}$

8.

Boy (B)   **Girl (G)**

```
      Boy (B)                    Girl (G)
     /      \                   /      \
    B        G                 B        G
   / \      / \               / \      / \
  B   G    B   G             B   G    B   G
```

9. 8

10a. $\dfrac{3}{8}$ b. $\dfrac{7}{8}$ c. $\dfrac{1}{8}$ d. $\dfrac{1}{2}$

e. $\dfrac{1}{2}$ f. $\dfrac{1}{2}$

11. No. The chance for the 4th child to be a boy or a girl is $\dfrac{1}{2}$.

12. $\dfrac{1}{3} ; \dfrac{1}{6} ; \dfrac{1}{3} ; \dfrac{1}{6} ; 0 ; 1$

13. 40 ; 20 ; 40 ; 20

Review Test

1. A   2. B   3. D   4. C
5. B   6. D   7. A   8. D
9. A

10.
```
        3 2 7
      ×   4 8
      -------
        2 6 1 6
    1 3 0 8 0
    -----------
    1 5 6 9 6
```

11.
```
          9 8 R5
    16 ) 1 5 7 3
         1 4 4
         -----
           1 3 3
           1 2 8
           -----
               5
```

12.
```
      0. 6 3 5
    8 ) 5. 0 8
        4 8
        ----
          2 8
          2 4
          ----
            4 0
            4 0
```

13. 1600

14. 32.606   15. 8.885   16. 5.356
17. 3297   18. 84   19. 115

20. $\dfrac{1}{3}$ 21. $\dfrac{11}{12}$

22. 0.6 ; 60% ; 3 : 5   23. $\dfrac{9}{20}$; 45% ; 9 : 20

24. $\dfrac{6}{25}$; 0.24 ; 6 : 25   25. $\dfrac{7}{20}$; 0.35 ; 35%

26. 6, 12, 18, 24, 30, 36, 42, 48, 54, 60 ;
    8, 16, 24, 32, 40, 48, 56, 64, 72, 80 ;
    24, 48 ; 24

27. 4, 8, 12, 16, 20, 24, 28, 32, 36, 40 ;
    5, 10, 15, 20, 25, 30, 35, 40, 45, 50 ;
    20, 40 ; 20
28. 1, 2, 3, 4, 6, 12   29. 1, 2, 4, 5, 10, 20
30. 1, 2, 3, 5, 6, 10, 15, 30   31. 1, 3, 5, 9, 15, 45
32. 4   33. 15   34. 6
35. 10   36. 68   37. 2 ; 3
38. 60   39. 3 ; 30   40. 12
41. 400   42. 80   43. 8000
44. 908.8   45. 75
46.

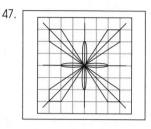

47.

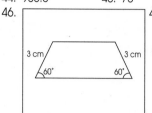

trapezoid

48.

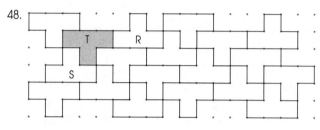

49 - 50. (Suggested answers for b.)
49a. Rotation
   b. Translate T; then reflect the translation image
50a. Rotation
   b. Reflect T; then translate the reflection image
51. 154, 154, 155, 157, 158, 160, 160, 161, 162, 166
52. 159
53. Taller children wear bigger shoes.

54a.

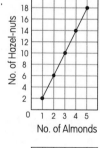

No. of Hazel-nuts vs No. of Almonds

   b. No. of hazel-nuts = No. of almonds x 4 – 2
   c. 30

55a.

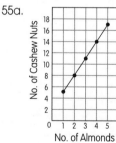

No. of Cashew Nuts vs No. of Almonds

   b. No. of cashew nuts = No. of almonds x 3 + 2
   c. 9